THE SAN EXPLORATORIUM

Written by Ruth Brown

Table of Contents

CelebrationPress

An Imprint of ScottForesman

What It Looks Like on the Outside ...

If you come to San Francisco, you might see a famous building called the Palace of Fine Arts. That's where you can find the Exploratorium.

The Palace was built for a huge fair in 1915. Afterwards, all the buildings from the fair were torn down except the Palace. People thought it was too beautiful to lose.

▼ **Panama Pacific Exposition, 1915**
In 1915, people came from all over the world to see the Panama Pacific Exposition. Can you find the Palace of Fine Arts in the picture? (It's all the way over on the left.)

But the building was so big, nobody knew what to do with it. The army put jeeps in it. The telephone company kept telephone books in it. People even played tennis in it.

Then, in 1969, it became a special kind of museum. Let's go inside and see.

What It's Really Like on the Inside ...

Have you ever been to a place where you can't touch anything or make any noise? That's not what the Exploratorium is like!

▲ **Inside the Museum**
More than half a million people come here every year.

At the Exploratorium, you can laugh as loud as you want. You can play with light, color, sound, electricity—just about anything you can think of. There are rainbows on the walls. There's a clock made of light.

You can make giant bubbles, leave your shadow on a wall, look inside an eye, or touch a tornado. This book will show you some of the amazing things you can do here.

▲ Machine Shop
You can look right into the Machine Shop and watch new exhibits being built.

All About You

Lots of Exploratorium exhibits help you find out interesting things about yourself—how you see, hear, even how you think. At one exhibit, people look like they're shrinking and growing when they walk around in a crooked room. They're not really changing—it's just what happens when your brain gets confused about what it's seeing.

▲ Find out how eyes work at the
Cow's Eye Dissection.

In the Life Sciences area, you can ride a special bike to find out how fast your heart beats. A skeleton in a closet lets you see what you'd look like without your skin on. You can even look inside a cow's eye. Sound yucky? Well, maybe a little. But it's pretty amazing too. Since a cow's eye works a lot like yours does, you can learn about how you see.

Did You Hear That?

Your ears may be funny to look at, but they're good at what they do. The cup-shaped outside collects sound. The hole in the middle lets the sound go deep inside your ear. Then your brain figures out what the sound is.

At the Exploratorium, there are lots of ways to experiment with sound and hearing. You can yell into a giant tube to make great echoes. You can make music on a computer. You can find out what happens when you try to listen to two people talking at the same time.

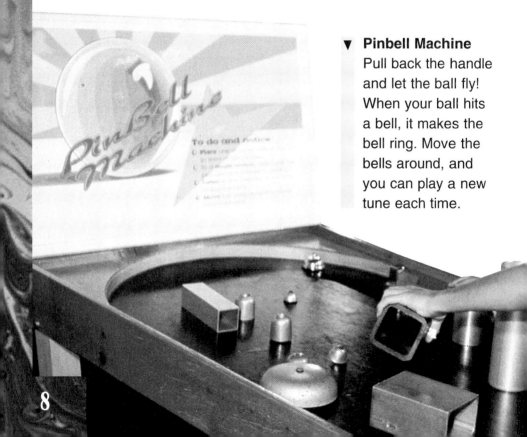

▼ **Pinbell Machine**
Pull back the handle and let the ball fly! When your ball hits a bell, it makes the bell ring. Move the bells around, and you can play a new tune each time.

▼ Pitch Switch

Turn the knob at this exhibit and you can make your voice sound as high as a chipmunk or as low as a giant.

Color Words

Here's a language game that might surprise you. Try saying the color that each word is printed in. Don't say the word! (For example, you should say "green" for the first word, not "red.")

RED LLOW LAV BLUE GREEN RED B
CK ORANGE LAVENDER PURPLE ORANGE P
LOW GREEN YELLOW LAVENDER PINK
UE GREEN BLUE GREEN
RED YELLOW ORANGE PINK
K ORANGE YELLOW
RED GREEN

How fast can you go? Sometimes kids are better at this than grown-ups. Try it on someone else and see how they do.

Hidden Pictures

At the Exploratorium, things aren't always what they seem.

▲ There are people hidden in this exhibit. Can you find them? (Hint: Look in the black spaces between the white columns.)

◀ There are two people here: an old lady and a young girl. Can you see them? (Hint: The young lady's necklace is the old woman's mouth. The young lady's chin is the old woman's nose.)

In the Land of the Ants

Could you be as small as an ant?
Could an ant grow as big as a person?
Only with the help of computers and
video cameras! Visit the exhibit called
In the Land of the Ants and see what
it's like to be in a different-sized world.

Magic Mirrors

Mirrors can do some pretty tricky things.

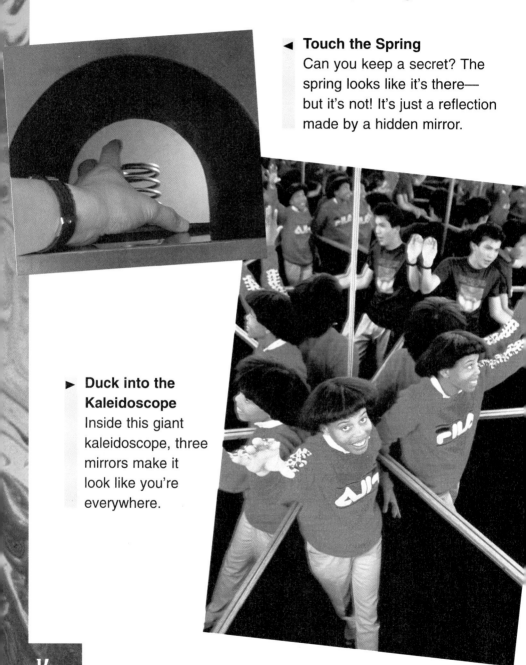

◀ **Touch the Spring**
Can you keep a secret? The spring looks like it's there— but it's not! It's just a reflection made by a hidden mirror.

▶ **Duck into the Kaleidoscope**
Inside this giant kaleidoscope, three mirrors make it look like you're everywhere.

▲ **Anti-Gravity Mirror**
If you stand at the edge of this mirror and flap your arm and leg, it looks like you can fly! If you have a mirror on a door at home, you can try this yourself.

Want to Try Some Mirror Tricks at Home?

Find a really shiny spoon and look at your reflection inside the bowl. Hey! How'd you get upside down? Now look on the back of the spoon. You're right side up again! Different-shaped spoons make different kinds of reflections.

Bubbles!

When you mix together soap and water,
not only do you get clean . . .
you also get bubbles!

▲ **Bubble Film Painting**
Did you ever notice the rainbow colors in a bubble? The
colors tell you how thick the bubble is. When the colors
go away and your bubble turns black—watch out!—it's
about to pop!

Want to Make Your Own Bubble Stuff?

You can make great bubbles at home by mixing a gallon of water with two-thirds of a cup of dish detergent. You'll get the best bubbles if you let the mixture sit a day.

► **Bubble Suspension**
Have you ever seen a frozen bubble? Bubbles are made out of soap and water. Sometimes, the water in a bubble can freeze into ice. At this exhibit, bubbles freeze when they touch a block of super-cold ice called "dry ice."

Shadows

Whenever you block the light, you make a shadow. At the Exploratorium, your shadow can be much more than a dark blob.

▼ **Colored Shadow Wall**
Here's a good place to rest. Sit on a bench and watch purple, pink, and green people walk by. Colored lights make rainbow shadows.

▲ **Recollections**
Dance inside Recollections and watch your shadow turn into a swirl of bright colors.

In the Dark

This is what the Tactile Dome looks like on the outside. ▼

This is what the Tactile Dome looks like on the inside. ►

You can't see anything because there's no light in the Tactile Dome. You have to find your way through its crazy maze using just your sense of touch.

Sorry we can't tell you more about it. It's a secret. But when you come here, you can feel what's inside!

Spinning Things

Did you ever wish you could spin around like an ice skater or a ballerina? Here's your chance!

Jump onto Momentum Machine, give yourself a push, and around you go. Stick out your leg to slow yourself down. Pull in your leg to speed up again. That's how spinning things work.

◀ Go for a spin on Momentum Machine.

You Never Know . . .

There are more than 700 exhibits at the Exploratorium. But you might come here on a day when something special is happening.

► When the Tibetan monks visited, they chanted sacred songs, drew beautiful pictures with colored sand, and made amazing sculptures out of butter. Really!

▼ People who came on Worm Day got to find out how wonderful the wiggly creatures could be.

There could be movies, or robot races, or a famous musician might be performing. You might be able to watch someone making a violin, weaving a basket, or tying sailors' knots. There might be a blacksmith giving a demonstration in one of the building's big old fireplaces. There could be jugglers or dancers or even TV stars to meet. You never know what might happen when you visit the Exploratorium!

▼ When the Cardoso Flea Circus came to town, visitors watched trained fleas jump out of miniature cannons and walk tiny tightropes.

Congratulations! You're a Scientist!

You don't have to go to a science museum to learn about science. Every time you think about how the world works, or notice something interesting, you're a scientist.

When you make shadow pictures on a wall, you're discovering how light works. When you bake cookies, you're experimenting with chemistry. When you ride a bike, you're finding out about how things move.

Science isn't just something you learn in school. It's a special way of thinking about the amazing world around you.